LGBTQ+ Dictionary

by **Matt Haslam**
Host of
Powered By Rainbows®

Index

80   Le$Bean
80   Leather
80   Lesbian
80   Lesbian Bed Death
80   Lesbian Labrys
81   Lesbophobia
81   LGBTQ
81   Librafluid
82   Lifestyle Choice
82   Lipstick Lesbian
82   Lithosexual
82   Lithromantic

M

84   M-Spec
84   MAAB / FAAB
84   Makkunrai
84   Manflux
84   Mascromantic
84   Mascsexual
84   Master-Slave
85   Maverique
85   Microlabel
85   Military Tribe
85   Minority Stress
86   Minus18
86   Misgender
86   Misogynoir
86   Mispronoun
86   Mixed Pronouns
87   MLM / MSM
87   Modifier
87   MOGA
88   MOGAI
88   Mono-Lesbian
88   Monogamous
88   Monolith
88   Monoromantive
89   Monosexism
89   Monosexual
89   MTF / M2F

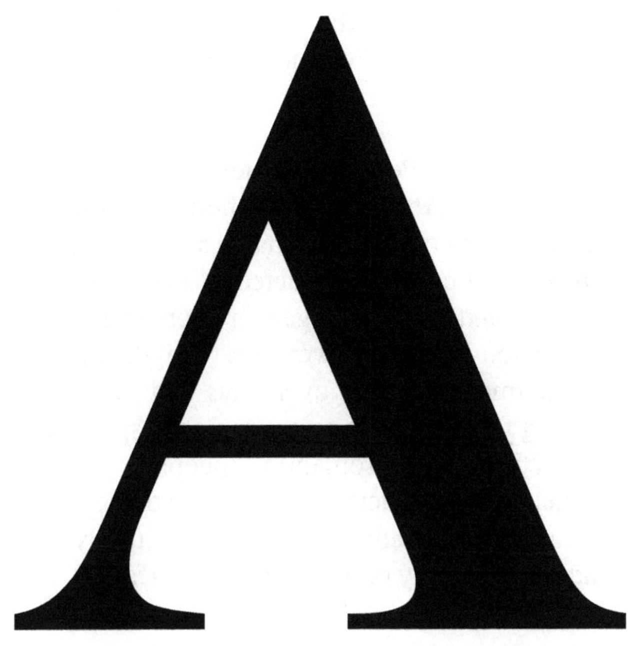

A-Spec – The asexual spectrum, sometimes abbreviated as A-Spec or aspec, refers to sexual orientations that are either asexual or on the asexual spectrum. For more information, please see *Asexual*.

A-Spectrum – This is the long-form way of saying *A-Spec* or aspec. For more information, please see *A-Spec*.

Abroromantic – People who define their romantic attraction as Abroromantic experience a romantic attraction to others that changes over time. This means you could be attracted to a certain gender today and another gender tomorrow. The attraction changes over any length of time, sometimes changing over days and other times taking years to move on the romantic spectrum of attraction. Abroromantic people are not romantically attracted to more than one gender at a time as their attraction changes entirely to be attracted to only one gender romantically.

Abrosexual – People who define their romantic attraction as Abrosexual experience a sexual attraction to others that changes over time. This means you could be attracted to a certain gender today and another gender tomorrow. The attraction changes over any length of time, sometimes changing over days and other times taking years to move on the sexual spectrum of attraction. Abrosexual people are not sexually attracted to more than one gender at a time as their attraction changes entirely to be attracted to only one gender sexually.

Ace – This is a nickname given to people who are *Asexual*. Rather than saying someone is on the Asexual Spectrum, you might refer to them or they might refer to themselves as Ace.

Ace Lesbian – This is one of many combination terms the LGBTQ community uses to better describe our members. Ace stands food a person who is *Asexual* and Lesbian is a term used to describe someone of the female gender being sexually, romantically, or otherwise attracted to the same gender. In the case of Ace Lesbian, because Ace means *Asexual*, it cancels out the sexual attraction we would normally define *Lesbian* with; therefore, an Ace Lesbian is someone of the female gender who is romantically or otherwise but not sexually attracted to people of the same gender.

Ace-Spec – This is another way of saying *A-Spec* or *A-Spectrum*. For more information, please see *A-Spec*.

AceAro – This term is used to describe someone who is *Asexual* or on the *Asexual Spectrum* and also *Aromantic* or on the *Aromantic Spectrum*. You might hear someone say they are AceAro or AroAce instead of saying they are *Aromantic* and *Asexual*. For more information, please see *Asexual* and *Aromantic*.

AceFlux – When someone is on the *Asexual Spectrum*, it means they are not sexually attracted to anyone of any gender. When that person's sexual attraction to one or more genders fluxuates (changes) over any length of time where one day they might be a tiny bit sexually attracted to one or more genders and another day, they are not sexually attracted to anyone of any gender, this is called AceFlux.

Acesexual – This term is used interchangeably with *Asexual*. Because the *Asexual* community uses *Ace* to describe themselves as a nickname rather than the longer-form *Asexual*, the community also combines their self-imposed nickname and their long-form term of sexual attraction for a combination term, Acesexual.

Achillean – This term refers to a person of the male gender or male-alligned genders who is attracted to other men and men-alligned genders. It is similar in definition to the term *MLM* or *Man Loving Men*.

Advocate – Someone who is not a member of the LGBTQIA+ community but uses their public protests and other methods in an attempt to improve the way LGBTQIA+ people live or minimize the challenges we face.

Aegoromantic / Autochorisromantic – A person who enjoys the idea of romance but does not wish to be a participant in romantic activities.

Aegosexual – This term was previously known as Autochorissexuality and is one of the many sexual orientations on the *Asexual Spectrum*. Similar to other Asexuals, people who identify as Aegosexual lack the desire to participate in sexual activites themselves; however, Aegosexuals have tendencies towards having sexual fantasies at times, despite having a disconnect between themselves and a sexual target or object of arousal.

AFAB – This abbreviation stands for Assigned Female at Birth. It is commonly used when describing a person's gender identity that does not match their sex assigned at birth.

Affirmed Gender – When someone is *Transgender*, the gender by which they wish to be known or described as is referred to as their Affirmed Gender. In the past, the LGBTQ community used terms like "new gender" or "chosen gender" which sometimes implied that their gender could be chosen or was not always their gender. So, to make the term more inclusive, we now use "Affirmed Gender" to describe the gender they wish to be known or described as.

AGAB – This abbreviation stands for Assigned Gender at Birth. It is used commonly among those that are *Transgender* to describe the gender they were wrongfully described as at birth but no longer wish to be associated with.

Agender – An individual who does not have a gender or has a lack of a gender identity. Agender people do not see themselves as male, female, non-binary, or any other gender identity. They are gender-neutral and often describe themselves as gender free or genderless.

Alexigender – An individual who identifies as Alexigender has a gender that is fluid between two genders. Those two genders are not known to the individual; however, the person knows their gender is fluid between multiple genders.

Allonormative – This describes the false belief that everyone, everywhere should experience sexual and romantic attraction to others. This belief marginalizes *Asexual* and *Aromantic* people for not being attracted to others and the Allonormative belief claims they should be attracted to others instead of being *Asexual* or *Aromantic*.

Alloromantic – This describes a person who feels romantic attraction to others. It does not matter if they are romantically attracted to people of the same gender or other genders.

Allosexual – This describes a person who feels sexual attraction to others. It does not matter if they are sexually attracted to people of the same gender or other genders.

Ally – This term describes a heterosexual (straight) and cisgender person who supports LGBTQ+ people of all sexual orientations and gender identities but does not belong to the community themselves.

Alphabet Mafia – Homophobic and transphobic people created the term "Alphabet Mafia" in an attempt to mock the LGBTQ community. The phrase is in reference to our community's name, LGBTQIA since it has so many letters. As with many names hate groups have called us over the years, the LGBTQ have now reclaimed this term and now use it as a badge of honor. So, it depends on the context it is used in on whether or not it is being used in a derogatory way.

AMAB – This abbreviation stands for Assigned Male at Birth. It is commonly used when describing a person's gender identity that does not match their sex assigned at birth.

Amatonormative – The assumption that everyone should have an exclusive romantic relationship no matter what. This belief marginalizes *polyamorous* people and those who wish to have multiple partners.

Androgyne – A person whose gender does not fit into the typical male or female gender roles or their gender is a mixture of male and female gender roles.

Androgynous – A person who defines their gender as *Androgyne*.

Androphilia – A term used in behavioral science to describe sexual orientation towards men or masculinity.

Androromantic – Someone who has a romantic attraction to men or masculinity.

Androsexual – Someone who has a sexual attraction to men or masculinity.

Angled AroAce – An individual who describes themselves as Angles AroAce has a romantic orientation close to *Aromantic* and on the *Aromantic Spectrum* but not entirely *Aromantic*. The individual will also have a sexual orientation close to *Asexual* and on the *Asexual Spectrum* but not entirely *Asexual*. For example, an Angled AroAce person can be *demisexual, demiromantic*, and so on.

Annual Reminder – Started in 1965, every year on July 4th, lesbian and gay people protested outside of Independence Hall in Philadelphia, PA, USA. They chose July 4th because that is Independence Day in the United States of America, the day the country claimed their independence and freedoms and became a country. Independence Hall is where the Declaration of Independence and U.S. Constitution were debated and signed. These documents gave every U.S. citizen the same equal rights under the law. But every July 4th starting in 1965, lesbian and gay people protested outside of this historic building on the most popular U.S. holiday to remind people that lesbian and gay people still do not have the same equal protections under the law nor do they have the same freedoms. In 1969, this "Annual Reminder" protest was overshadowed by the Stonewall Riots which would later become the Christopher Street Liberation Day and later be known as Pride Month in June.

Aphobia – A hatred or prejudice to *Asexual* and *Aromantic* people.

Aplatonic – Sometimes abbreviated as Apl (pronounced Apple), this term describes someone who does not wish to have an intimate or affectionate relationship with anyone.

Aporagender – This is a non-binary gender identity which is an umbrella term for a person whose gender is separate from male, female, or anything in between. They still have a gender, unlike *Agender*, but it is separate from male, female, and anything in between.

Aro – An abbreviation for someone on the *Aromantic Spectrum*.

Aro-Spec – An abbreviation of the term *Aromantic Spectrum*

AroAce – Someone who is both *Aromantic* and *Asexual* might use this abbreviation to describe their orientations.

Aroflux – Someone whose romantic orientation fluctuates over any length of time but generally stays on the *Aromantic Spectrum*.

Aromantic – A person who experiences little to no romantic attraction to others.

Aromantic Spectrum – This term refers to the romantic orientations that are *Aromantic* or are closely associated with *Aromantic*.

Asexual – A person who experiences little to no sexual attraction to others.

Asexual Biromantic – Someone who experiences little to no sexual attraction to others and experiences romantic attraction to two genders.

Asexual Panromantic – Someone who experiences little to no sexual attraction to others but is romantically attracted to people regardless of gender.

Asexual Spectrum – This term refers to the sexual orientations that are *Asexual* or are closely associated with *Asexual*.

Aspec – This is an abbreviation of the term *Asexual Spectrum*.

Assigned Gender – Typically used when speaking about *transgender* gender identities, Assigned Gender refers to the gender someone was assigned at birth by their parents or doctors. It is an abbreviated way of saying Assigned Gender at Birth or *AGAB*.

Assumed Gender – The gender others assume you are from your *gender expression*. For example, if you wear clothing typically associated with females, others would assume your gender is on the feminine side of the *gender spectrum*.

Autochorissexual – This is an old term that has now been replaced with *Aegosexual*.

Autoromantic – Someone who is romantically attracted to themselves.

Autosexual – Someone who is sexually attracted to themselves.

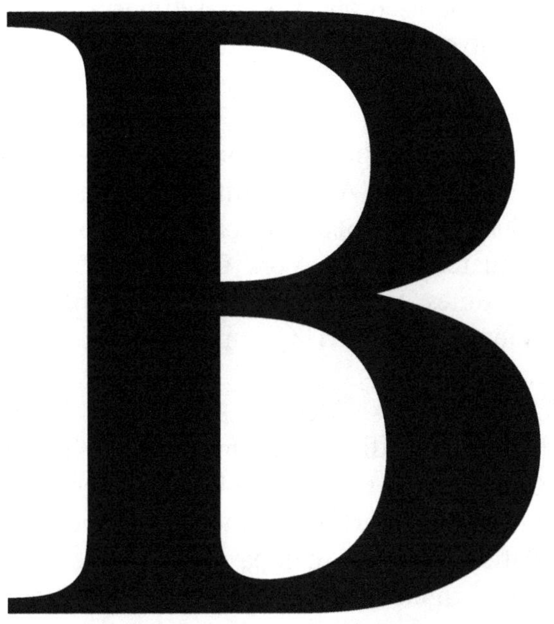

Baby Dyke – This term describes a young lesbian; however, the term Dyke can be highly offensive since it originally was a slur homophobic people used in a derogatory way against lesbians and has now been reclaimed. So, while the term Baby Dyke technically describes a young lesbian, it should be used on in select settings as to not be offensive.

Ballroom Culture – Also known as the Ballroom Scene or Ballroom Community, this term describes an African-American and Latino underground subculture for LGBTQ people that originated in New York City, NY, USA. It is sometimes used when describing black and Latinos in the LGBTQ community.

BDSM Rights – BDSM stands for bondage, discipline, sadism, and masochism. The term BDSM Rights refers to the belief that people who enjoy or want BDSM practices in their sexual relationships with their partners deserve the same human rights as everyone else. It also describes the belief that they should not be discriminated against for pursuing BDSM with consenting adults.

Bear – While in everyday life, this term describes an actual animal in nature; in the LGBTQ community, this term describes a larger and often-times hairier man or masculine gendered person who projects an image of rugged masculinity.

Bear Tribe – This term is used to describe the overall community of people who are *Bears*. At a Pride event or an LGBTQ hangout spot, rather than saying "there's a couple of bears over there" which might scare people who might be frightened at animals who can harm them, you would say "there's the Bear Tribe over there."

Beard – If someone is not out of the closet as LGBTQ or they are afraid of others in close proximity knowing they belong to the LGBTQ, they might use what is called a Beard. In everyday life, a Beard is something typically on the face of a masculine gendered person (hiding their chin from other people's view); however, in our community Beard stands for something much different and can describe someone of any gender. Beard is a person who is knowingly or unknowingly used to conceal or cover up someone's sexual orientation. For example, if you were young and didn't want your parents to find out you are gay, you might date someone of an opposite gender to throw them off. If you lived in a homophobic country, a lesbian couple and a gay couple might present themselves as dating in heterosexual relationships to appease government or law enforcement officials. Both of these situations would be best described as having a Beard.

Bellusromantic – This term describes a portion of the *Aromantic Spectrum* where the person has an interest in traditionally romantic things such as kissing or cuddling but they do not feel romantic attraction nor do they want a romantic relationship.

Bi-Gay – Someone who is *Bisexual* but leans more towards their attraction to their same gender. Usually, Bi-Gay refers to someone of masculine gender identities.

Bi-Lesbian – Someone who is *Bisexual* but leans more towards their attraction to the same gender. Usually, Bi-Lesbian refers to someone of feminine gender identities.

Bicon – This term refers to someone who is a *Bisexual* icon like a well-known person in the bisexual community or a celebrity who happens to also be bisexual.

Bigender – Someone with exactly two gender identities.

Bigender Pansexual – Someone with exactly two gender identities and someone who is sexually attracted to other people regardless of those other peoples' gender identities.

Binary – The incorrect social belief that there are only two classifications of gender – male or female.

Binary Gender – Similar to *Binary*, this is the incorrect social belief that there are only two classifications of gender – male and female.

Binder – An article of clothing that tightly fits around a person's chest area to bind their breasts as an alternative to or while waiting for *top surgery*. Binders are typically used by *Transgender* men and *Non-Binary* individuals.

Binding – The act of using a *Binder*.

Bioessentialism – This term is short for biological essentialism. It refers to the reliance or weaponization of biology in an attempt to disprove trans people's genders. Common bioessentialist arguments reduce people to their chromosomes (though there are more than 30 chromosome combinations that people have); their genitalia (though there are many natural variations); or their binary gender (though gender and sex are not binary).

Biphobia – The fear of, discrimination against, or hatred of *Bisexual* people or those who are perceived as such.

BIPOC – This term is the abbreviation for a *Bisexual* person of color.

Biromantic – A person who is romantically attracted to two genders.

Biromantic Demisexual – A person who is romantically attracted to two genders; however, they are only sexually attracted to others once an emotional connection is formed between them.

Biromantic Homosexual – A person who is romantically attracted to two genders; however, is only sexually attracted to people of the same gender.

Bisexual – A person who is sexually attracted to two genders.

Bisexual Bigender – A person who is sexually attracted to two genders; however, they also have two gender identities themselves. The two genders they are attracted to do not have to be the same genders they identify as.

Bisexual Panromantic – Someone who is sexually attracted to two genders; however, they are romantically attracted to other people regardless of their gender.

Bissu – This term refers to the Indonesian ethnic group where Bissu is one of the five genders of the Bugis. In the LGBTQ community, we have used this term to describe someone who is considered neither male nor female but representative of the totality of the *gender spectrum*.

Boi – This term describes a number of groups in the LGBTQ community. One of them being a boyish lesbian. Another being a submissive butch lesbian in the BDSM community. A third being a young transgender man or a transgender man in the early stages of transitioning.

Bottom – A term used to describe a person's desire or ability to receive their partner's body parts inside of them during intercourse in a gay relationship.

Bottom Surgery – Surgery performed on an individual's reproductive system as a part of gender-affirming surgery. Not all transgender people undergo medical interventions as part of their transition. As with any other aspect of transition, trans people retain the right not to discuss their surgical history, and surgery does not define gender.

Boyflux – A subgroup of gender identity where someone has a male gender identity most of the time but also experiences varying degrees of masculinity.

Breeder – A derogatory term used by LGBTQ people to describe heterosexual / straight people.

Bulldagger – Most often, this term is used in a derogatory way to describe a masculine lesbian. It is most often heard in African American communities.

Butch – A person who identifies themselves as masculine, whether it be physically, mentally, or emotionally. 'Butch' is sometimes used as a derogatory term for lesbians but it was also reclaimed as an affirmative identity label by the lesbian community. Whether the term is derogatory or not depends on the context of the sentence it is used in and by whom it is used by.

Butch Lesbian Tribe – A group of lesbians who present and identify themselves as *Butch*.

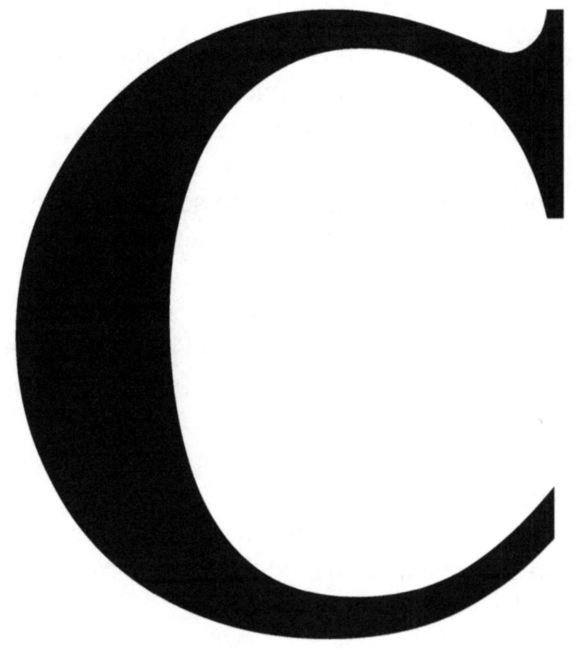

Calabai – This term refers to the Indonesian ethnic group where Calabai is one of the five genders of the Bugis. Calabai is someone who is born with a male body but take on female gender roles such as wearing dresses, makeup, and growing their hair long.

Calalai – This term refers to the Indonesian ethnic group where Calalai is one of the five genders of the Bugis. Calalai is someone who is born with a female body but take on traditionally male gender roles such as wearing shirts, trousers, cut their hair shorter, and work manual jobs.

Ceteroromantic – Sometimes referred to as *skolioromantic*, someone who is Ceteroromantic experiences a romantic attraction to *Non-Binary* gender identities.

Ceterosexual – Sometimes referred to as *skoliosexual*, someone who is Ceterosexual experiences a sexual attraction to *Non-Binary* gender identities.

Chosen Family – When you are LGBTQ, sometimes in worst-case scenarios, your biological family does not accept you for being who you are and loving the way you love. So, the LGBTQ community takes on this family role and loves you like you were our own family member. We refer to this as being your Chosen Family because biological families can sometimes be homophobic or transphobic but Chosen Families are always accepting.

Cis – An abbreviated way to say *Cisgender*.

Cisgender – A person whose gender identity and assigned sex at birth correspond. For example, a person who is not *transgender*.

Cisgender Heterosexual – A person who is not *transgender* and they are only attracted to people of an opposite gender. This is a scientific way to describe those that do not belong to the LGBTQ community.

Cishet – A sometimes derogatory way to describe someone outside the LGBTQ community. It is an abbreviated way to say *Cisgender Heterosexual*.

Cisnormative – The incorrect belief that everyone is cisgender and that transgender people do not exist. It is the belief that only male and female genders are the only two gender options and that gender cannot exist on a spectrum of identities. People who believe in a Cisnormative society do not follow logic or science in order to get to their conclusions or beliefs…because obviously Transgender people exist and gender is on a spectrum.

Cissexism – This term describes the prejudice, towards transgender people. It is the false belief that gender and sex are the same; and therefore, there must only be two genders.

Closeted – Describes a person who is not open about their sexual orientation or gender identity. A closeted person may be referred to as being "in the closet." There are many degrees to being closeted or out of the closet. For example, closeted individuals may be out to just themselves, close friends, or to their larger network, or not publicly open about their status as LGBTQ.

Coming Out – The process by which one accepts and/or comes to identify one's own sexual orientation or gender identity. It is most often used to describe the act of telling other people their sexual orientation or gender identity but is also a term used to describe the self-realization of your sexual orientation or gender identity. In other words, you can come out to yourself in the mirror and realize you are LGBTQ before coming out to anyone else.

Comphet – The abbreviated way to say *Compulsory Heterosexuality*.

Compulsory Heterosexuality – The theory that heterosexuality (being straight) is assumed and enforced upon everyone as a child. This forces people of other sexual orientations to "come out" later in life against the patriarchal norm that society says everyone has to be straight.

Constellation – A way to describe the arrangement or structure of a *polyamorous* relationship.

Cottage Core Lesbian – A lesbian who likes earthly things such as planting flowers or bee keeping.

Cub – A younger or younger looking version of a *Bear*.

Culture Specific Identities – A sexual orientation or gender identity that is exclusive to a particular culture and does not have an equivalent in another culture elsewhere in the world.

Cupioromantic – A person who desires a romantic relationship but does not experience romantic attraction to others.

Deadname – This refers to the name someone was assigned at birth but a name they have since chosen to no longer be called. Some may prefer the terms birth name, given name, or old name.

Deadnaming – Occurs when an individual, intentionally or not, refers to the name that a transgender or gender-expansive individual used at a different time in their life. Deadnaming someone, intentionally or not, is a derogatory way to describe them which reduces their gender and lets them know you don't think their gender is valid, which of course it is valid. So, please avoid this practice, as it can cause trauma, stress, embarrassment, and even danger.

Demi Bisexual – A person who is sexually attracted to two genders but only after an emotional bond is formed between them.

Demiboy – A person whose gender identity is on the gender spectrum between *Agender* and male.

Demiflux – A person whose gender identity has parts that fluctuate in intensity and other parts are static (remain the same).

Demigender – A person whose gender identity partially ties to a specific gender identity or idea of gender but is not fully connected to that identity.

Demigirl – A person whose gender identity is on the gender spectrum between *Agender* and female.

Demiromantic – A person whose romantic attraction to others only forms once an emotional bond is formed between them.

Demisexual – A person whose sexual attraction to others only forms once an emotional bond is formed between them.

Demisexual Gay – A person who is only sexually attracted to those of the same gender but that sexual attraction only forms once an emotional bond is formed between them.

Demisexual Panromantic – A person who is only sexually attracted to others once an emotional bond is formed; however, they are romantically attracted to others regardless of gender.

Demisexual Pansexual – A person who is only sexually attracted to others once an emotional bond is formed; however, they could be sexually attracted to any person regardless of gender.

Diamoric – When a *Non-Binary* or *gender-expansive* person is attracted to a person with a feminine gender identity, it is called Diamoric.

Disclosure – While *Coming Out* is a term we use for a person telling themselves or others that their sexual orientation is anything other than heterosexual (straight), Disclosure is the term used to describe when a transgender or Non-Binary person tells others their gender identity is different than their sex assigned at birth.

Discrimination – This term is used to describe the prejudice and power over someone else or a minority group. It occurs when members of a more powerful social group behave unjustly or cruelly to members of a less powerful social group. Discrimination can take many forms, including both individual acts of hatred of injustice and institutional denials of privileges normally accorded to other groups. Ongoing discrimination creates a climate of oppression for the affected group.

Do You Listen to Girl in Red? – This is a code word question usually asked by a lesbian to figure out if the person they are talking to is also a lesbian. If you answer yes, you are signaling to the other person that you are in fact a lesbian.

DOMA – This is an abbreviation of the term Defense of Marriage Act which was a discriminatory law in 1996 barring LGBTQ people from getting married in the United States. It has since been overturned but the basis of it was to 'defend' marriage between one man and one woman…because LGBTQ people getting equal rights and protections under the law was scary for some people in 1996.

Don't Say Gay – A bill or a law that is proposed or passed to silence LGBTQ people and voices. For example, in 2023 the state of Florida in the United States passed a law that would ban any teacher from talking about any sexual orientation or gender identity in classrooms in Preschool to third grade. It was done to stop LGBTQ people from being represented and stop LGBTQ children from feeling normal or accepted by their teachers and peers. But it many times leads to every school, no matter the grade level from talking about LGBTQ people at all. Because of the way these laws are worded (to protect the lawmakers from being accused of suppressing free speech), they end up banning heterosexual and cisgender talk in schools too. These bills and laws severely limit the education those states can provide because it's very difficult to teach any history, literature, or even have a library in a school without mentioning any words that even relate to gender or sexual orientation so the ones who suffer the most from these bills and laws are the students.

Drag – This term first came about in the times of the famous playwriter William Shakespeare who lived from April 1564 to April 1616. Back in those days, women could not be a part of plays or act on a public stage so men had to play women's roles on stage. Shakespeare would write the abbreviation DRAG in his scripts standing for Dressed Resembling A Girl. Today, the term survives as a way for someone to perform one or multiple genders theatrically. Those who perform are called Drag Kings and Drag Queens.

Drag King – A person who consciously performs "masculinity," usually in a show or theatre setting, presenting an exaggerated form of masculine expression, often times done by a woman. This term is often confused with "transsexual" or "transvestite." Drag may be performed as a political comment on gender, as parody, or simply as entertainment. Drag performance does not indicate sexuality, gender identity, or sex identity.

Drag Pageantry – This is a more refined style of drag performance for female impersonators, *Drag Queens*, and transgender women. It is modelled after beauty pageants and contests.

Drag Queen – A person who consciously performs "femininity," usually in a show or theatre setting, presenting an exaggerated form of feminine expression, often times done by a man. Again, this term is often confused with "transsexual" or "transvestite." Drag may be performed as a political comment on gender, as parody, or simply as entertainment. Drag performance does not indicate sexuality, gender identity, or sex identity.

Dyke – This is a derogatory term referring to a masculine lesbian. The term has since been reclaimed by some lesbians as a positive word when describing themselves, but generally this is a derogatory term that should not be used.

Egogender – A gender identity in which the person who identifies as Egogender has a gender identity that is specific to them and only them. They identify their gender simply as oneself.

Enbian – This is a sexual orientation which describes a *Non-Binary* individual who is only attracted to and only is interested in relationships with other *Non-Binary* individuals.

Enby – This is an abbreviation used for a *Non-Binary* person in the LGBTQ community. It's a phonetic pronunciation of NB, short for Non-Binary, or people who do not identify their gender as male or female.

Equality – The term "Equality" (in the context of diversity) is typically defined as treating everyone the same and giving everyone access to the same opportunities. It is sometimes used as an alternative to "inclusion".

Faggot / Fag – This is an extremely derogatory term referring to a gay person, or someone perceived as queer. While often used derogatorily, it is also sometimes used by gay men to describe themselves but should not be used by anyone under any circumstances because of the word's history and extreme negative connotation. In the United Kingdom, this term describes a cigarette but to the rest of the world, this is an extremely derogatory term.

Fat Tribe – Sometimes referred to as the Cubby Culture, this group in the LGBTQ is made up of people who are overweight or obese gay men who self-identify as part of the Fat Tribe. While most people assume this is a derogatory way to describe people, people who self-identify as part of this tribe (or group) consider it to be a celebration of who they are and celebration of being happy with the body they live in.

Feminine – A set of behaviors, presentations, and roles that are associated with being a woman.

Femme – A person who is feminine of center in dress, attitude, and/or presentation. It is often, but not exclusively, used in a lesbian context.

Femromantic – A romantic orientation in which the person is only attracted to those of feminine gender identities.

Femsexual – A sexual orientation in which the person is only attracted to those of feminine gender identities.

Fetish – A sexual attraction to something that is nonsexual or attracted to something to a more extreme degree than most other people.

Flawless Sabrina – In the 1960's, Flawless Sabrina was a pioneer for transgender and drag queens who were being persecuted in those days in the United States. Sabrina lived in New York City, USA near Central Park and was a major icon of the decade. Nowadays, you might hear the term Flawless Sabrina being cheered at Pride events or around current transgender and drag activists as a way to support their cause and call them a pioneer for helping the LGBTQ community.

Fluidflux – A gender identity where the person's gender changes over time while at the same time varying in intensity.

Frayromantic – A romantic orientation where the person only experiences a romantic attraction to someone they are not deeply connected with. You could think of this as they are only romantically attracted to those that they are far away from or on the fray with.

Fraysexual - A sexual orientation where the person only experiences a sexual attraction to someone they are not deeply connected with. You could think of this as they are only sexually attracted to those that they are far away from or on the fray with.

Fruity – A fairly new term created by the LGBTQ community to describe a gay person.

FTM / F2M – A transgender person whose gender identity is male, may use these terms to describe themselves. Some will just use the term man which is equally as valid.

FTX / F2X – A genderqueer or gender-expansive person assigned female at birth.

Furry – A person who is an enthusiast for animal characters with human characteristics. Usually a furry is a person who dresses in a costume resembling an animal character or uses an animal character as an online avatar. Not all furries are LGBTQ and not all LGBTQ people are furries. While some people are fearful of furries, there is absolutely nothing to be fearful of and people who identify as furries are completely healthy and normal. This is not to be confused with gender identity or sexual orientation seeing that being a furry is not a sexual orientation nor is it a gender identity.

Gatekeeping – A broad term, not only used within the LGBTQ+ community, which describes the process by which an individual decides who does or does not belong to a certain community, group, or identity. For example, a gay man telling a questioning man that he has to have sex with another man before he can call himself gay is an example of gatekeeping. Gatekeeping, which can come from inside or outside the LGBTQ+ community should be avoided, as it is painful and invalidating to the recipient in either instance.

Gay – A person who is attracted to people of the same gender, otherwise known as homosexual. Sometimes the word Gay can be used as an insult to our community when it is yelled from a homophobic person. So, whether it is used in a derogatory way or a positive way is determined by how it is used in a sentence and by whom it is said by.

Gay Agenda – A derogatory term used by those who hate the LGBTQ community and a term that falsely accuses the community of having a hidden motivation of hatred. In truth, the LGBTQ have since reclaimed this term a little bit, because if we did have an agenda, it would be one of love and acceptance.

Gay Male – A person with a male or masculine gender identity who is only attracted to other males.

Gayby – A person with one or more LGBTQ parents or caregivers. Typically, this term is used for self-identification only.

Gaydar – The ability to tell if someone is gay just by looking at them. The word combines the words gay and radar.

Geek Tribe – A group in the LGBTQ community that are more technically savvy and love to build and use computers or related devices. This is not a sexual orientation or gender identity but rather a community inside the LGBTQ that are proud to call themselves 'geeks.'

Gender – The socially constructed set of characteristics of norms, behaviors, and roles that are typically associated with being a woman, man, Non-Binary, or gender-expansive person. Because it is a socially constructed set of characteristics, it can change over time from one society to the next.

Gender Alignment – A term to describe where your gender is on the gender identity spectrum. For example, this term can be used to describe which gender you are aligned with the most.

Gender Apathy – A person who does not care what gender identity they are and have never thought too much about what their answer would be if they were asked what gender they identify with.

Gender Binary – The false belief that there are only two genders, male and female. This term is used mostly by *Non-Binary* individuals to describe that their gender identity fits outside of the Gender Binary.

Gender Critical Feminism – A fairly new term to describe anti-transgender activists, transphobic people, and hate groups focused on excluding trans women from being included in definitions regarding women. For example, people who are hell-bent on excluding trans women from women sporting programs or women bathrooms.

Gender Dysphoria – When a transgender person's appearance is different from their gender identity, it may cause them stress. This stress is sometimes referred to as Gender Dysphoria. For example, when a trans woman looks in the mirror, she might feel stress about not looking like other women with breasts. This causes her stress which is called Gender Dysphoria.

Gender Essentialism – The false belief that men have to be dominant and women have to be submissive. For the LGBTQ, this belief becomes the keystone of the argument against being homosexual, bisexual, and any other sexuality other than heterosexual (straight) because Gender Essentialism is the belief that in a relationship, there has to be one man who is dominant and one woman that is submissive.

Gender Euphoria – A great feeling often experienced when one's gender is recognized and respected by others, when one's body aligns with one's gender, or when one expresses themselves in accordance with their gender. Focusing on gender euphoria instead of gender dysphoria shifts focus towards the positive aspects of being transgender or gender expansive.

Gender Expansive – This term is used to describe people whose gender identity is outside the gender spectrum. It is sometimes used by Non-Binary, genderfluid, and other gendered individuals; however, it is mostly used by people whose gender identity is flexible and changes over time.

Gender Expression – The way a person acts, dresses, speaks, and behaves. For example, feminine, masculine, or androgynous. Gender expression does not necessarily correspond to assigned sex at birth or gender identity.

Gender Fluid – A person whose *gender expression* changes over time or whose gender expression has multiple aspects of many different gender identities simultaneously.

Gender Fluid Abrosexual – A person whose gender expression and sexual orientation changes over any length of time.

Gender Fluid Gay – A person's whose gender expression can change over any length of time; however, their sexual orientation remains constant and they are always attracted to people of the same gender.

Gender Identity – A person's internal sense of being a male, female, both, neither, fluid on the gender spectrum, or another gender.

Gender Modality – This term describes how closely the gender someone identifies as compared to their gender assigned at birth.

Gender Neutral – The complete absence of gender.

Gender Non-Conforming – A person who does not conform or meet the gender norms that are expected of them by society.

Gender Performance Theory – The incorrect theory that any other gender besides male or female is not natural, even though many scientific studies and laws prove other genders are valid. This false belief says that every other gender besides male and female are simply a 'performance'.

Gender Presentation – Another term for *Gender Expression*.

Gender Queer – An umbrella term with a similar meaning to *Non-Binary*. It means someone's gender identity is outside the binary spectrum and not male or female.

Gender Questioning – Someone who is questioning or trying to figure out what their gender identity is.

Gender Socialization – The process by which parents, guardians, and others teach children how they should behave as male or female. This is done in many ways including forcing boys to like certain toys or painting their room blue and forcing girls to wear dresses or painting their rooms pink. This is yet another hurdle transgender and gender-expansive individuals have to overcome when questioning their gender when in truth, a perfect society would not have such a Gender Socialization forcing kids to think there are only two genders.

Gender Spectrum – The concept that gender exists beyond a simple man and woman binary model, but instead exists on a spectrum. Some people fall towards more masculine or feminine aspects, some people move fluidly along the spectrum, and some exist off the spectrum entirely.

Genderfae – A gender identity which is fluid between many different genders but is never male or male-aligned.

Genderfaun – A gender identity which is fluid between many different genders but is never female or female-aligned.

Genderflor – A gender identity which is fluid between many different genders but is never male, female, male-aligned, or female-aligned.

Genderflux – A person whose gender identity experiences a range in intensity over any length of time.

Genderfuck – This term describes the actions of gender non-conforming individuals take in order to rebel against the restrictive societal roles put on gender.

Genderless – Another term for Agender, meaning not having a gender.

Gendervague – This term was first created within the autistic community and it defines a person who cannot separate their gender identity from their neurodivergence.

Gendervoid – A complete lack of experience associated with any gender identity.

Girlflux – A person whose gender identity is on the feminine side of the gender spectrum but whose gender fluctuates in intensity.

GLBT – Another way of saying LGBT but this time with the acronym in the order of Gay, Lesbian, Bisexual and Transgender.

GLG – An acronym meaning Girl Loving other Girls. This is the much more inclusive way to describe women being homosexual.

GNC – An abbreviation of the term *Gender Non-Conforming*.

Gold Star Gay / Gold Star Lesbian – A term used to describe a gay person who has never been with or had sexual intercourse with a straight partner.

Gray Agender – A person whose gender identity is outside the gender binary and they have very mixed feelings on how their gender should be defined.

Gray Asexual – An orientation on the sexual orientation spectrum somewhere between *Asexual* and another sexual orientation where the person only experiences sexual attraction on occasion.

Grayromantic – Similar to *Aromantic*, being Grayromantic means a person is not romantically attracted to any gender. Unlike *Aromantic* though, Grayromantic individuals are romantically attracted to others on a rare occasion.

Graysexual – Similar to *Asexual*, being Graysexual means a person is not sexually attracted to any gender. Unlike *Asexual* though, Graysexual individuals are sexually attracted to others on a rare occasion.

Grey Pansexual – A person who is only sometimes sexually attracted to others; however, when they are sexually attracted to others, they are attracted to them regardless of gender.

Greysexual – A person who is rarely attracted to other people regardless of gender.

Gynephilia – A sexual orientation meaning someone is sexually attracted to women or femininity.

Gyneromantic – A romantic orientation meaning someone is romantically attracted to women or femininity.

Gynesexual – A sexual orientation meaning someone is attracted sexually to female anatomy, regardless of the person they are attracted to identifying as a woman or on the feminine side of the gender spectrum.

Gynoromantic – A romantic orientation meaning someone is romantically attracted to women or femininity.

Gynosexual – A sexual orientation meaning someone is sexually attracted to women or femininity.

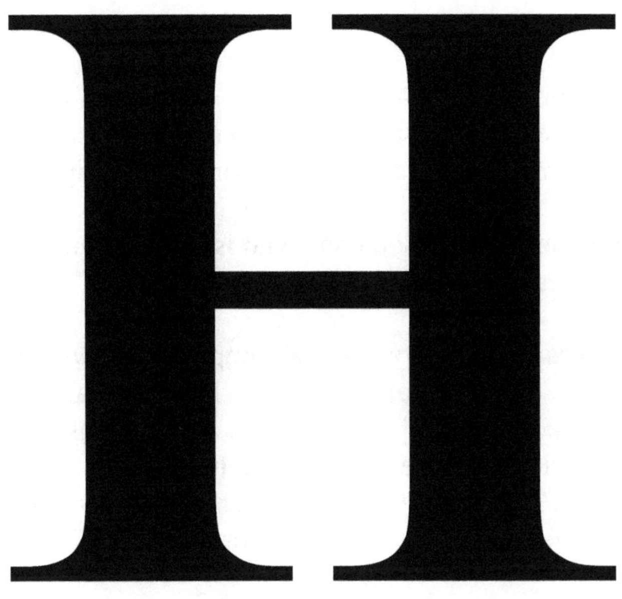

Hermaphrodite – This term is the very old way of describing an *Intersex* person. It was used in a derogatory way to refer to Intersex people but has since been reclaimed by the Intersex community to showcase their pride. Use of this term should be avoided in most cases and nowadays, we use the word Intersex which is a lot more inclusive.

Heteroflexible – Someone who is mostly heterosexual (straight) but sometimes encounters homosexual (gay) activities or relationships.

Heteromantic – Someone who is only romantically attracted to people of an opposite gender.

Heteronormativity – The assumption that everyone is heterosexual and that heterosexuality is superior to all other sexual orientations. This includes the often-implied idea that heterosexuality is the norm and that other sexual orientations are "different" or "abnormal."

Herosexism – Sometimes referred to as homophobia, Herosexism is the belief that only relationships with one man and one woman should be allowed in society.

Heterosexual – Most times this term is used interchangeably with the word 'Straight'. Heterosexual means someone is only attracted to one gender besides their own gender. While many homophobic people believe this means one man and one woman, that is far from the case. In truth, heterosexual relationships can include a transgender person (for example: A trans-man in a relationship with a woman) or a person of another gender (for example: A woman in a relationship with a Non-Binary individual). Both of these examples are considered heterosexual relationships because they are a person with one gender identity in a relationship with someone of a different gender identity.

Hijra – In the Indian culture, rather than someone identifying as transgender, they would instead identify as Hijra meaning not male or female but instead, a third gender.

Homoflexible – Someone who is mostly homosexual (gay) but sometimes encounters heterosexual (straight) activities or relationships.

Homophobia – The fear of, discrimination against, or hatred of lesbian or gay people or those who are perceived as such.

Homoromantic – Someone who is romantically attracted to people of the same gender.

Homosexual – Someone who is sexually attracted to people of the same gender.

Hormone Blockers – Sometimes called Puberty Blockers, Hormone Blockers are prescribed by licensed doctors to help transgender youth transition to their actual gender identity. These decrease the intensity of puberty for teenagers which helps them have a smoother transition to their actual gender as an adult. Most hormone blockers are completely reversible and perfectly safe.

Hormone Replacement Therapy – Otherwise known as HRT, this is a treatment which allows transgender and gender-expansive people to medically transition or feel more at home in their bodies. Those taking testosterone (masculine hormones) may grow more facial and body hair and notice their voices deepening. Those taking estrogen (feminizing hormones) may see some breast growth and decreased libido. Many intersex people take HRT to balance the naturally occurring levels of estrogen and testosterone in their bodies. Benefits of such therapy can include improved mental and physical wellness, and reduced anxiety and dysphoria, for those who experience it.

House-Ballroom Community – Another term used interchangeably with *Ballroom Community*.

HRT – An abbreviation of *Hormone Replacement Therapy*.

Hyperfemininity – An over exaggeration of female characteristics and behavior society normally associates with famine gender identities.

Hypermasculinity – An over exaggeration of male characteristics and behavior society normally associates with masculine gender identities.

I

Ignotasexual – A person who is more sexually attracted to a person they just met as compared to a person they have known for a long time.

IMOGA – Another abbreviation used interchangeably with *MOGAI*. IMOGA stands for Intersex, Marginalized Orientations, and Gender Alignments.

Intergender – A variation of characteristics in a person's DNA and/or genitalia that does not allow them to be assigned male or female at birth.

Internalized Homophobia – The conscious or unconscious belief a homosexual (gay or lesbian) person has in the lies homophobic people tell about homosexuals. For example, a gay person might be taught all throughout their childhood that marriage is between a man and a woman or that being gay is a sin in the eyes of their religion (which are both false) but these are things that person will have to overcome later in life before coming out or having relationships they are meant to be in. Homophobic teachings early in life to children do serious damage to LGBTQ people for years to come which is why an accepting home life, school, church, and community are vital for all children.

Intersectionality – This term refers to the common overlaps in oppression and fight for equal rights between different communities. For example, in the United States many laws discriminating and marginalizing African Americans were the same laws oppressing LGBTQ people; therefore, many of the protests to get rid of this discrimination had both communities in attendance to fight back and get the laws repealed. Similarly, the transgender community has always fought for the equal rights and protections under the law for gay, lesbian, bisexual, and other orientations. They have in turn protested on behalf of the transgender and gender-expansive community for equal rights. Intersectionality means we all stick together to hopefully bring change and equality faster to our communities.

Intersex – A person who is born with characteristics not typically associated with male or female or these characteristics develop naturally during puberty.

Kinsey Scale – An outdated scale developed in the 1940s by Alfred Kinsey which places an individual's sexual orientation on a spectrum from 0 (meaning exclusively heterosexual) to 6 (exclusively homosexual). The scale included the measurement "X" which indicated an absence of sexual behavior. The scale was an early recognition of fluid sexual orientation and was credited with challenging the heterosexual and homosexual binary. Nowadays, the Kinsey Scale is no longer used to describe sexual orientation and we have since replaced the scale with 7 spectrums of orientation. This is because 7 spectrums rather than one scale can better describe the full spectrum of how a person can love in different categories.

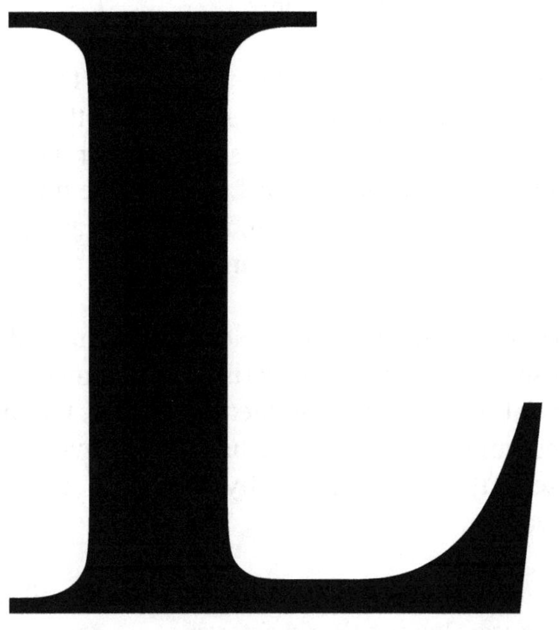

Latinx – A person of Latin-American decent who does not identify as either male or female.

Le$Bean – A term used by lesbians to fool TikTok and other social media websites from flagging the word *lesbian* and suppressing LGBTQ content from public view.

Leather – Sometimes called the Leather Tribe, this term refers to the practice of using clothing such as jackets, boots, harnesses, or other items in sexual activities. Not all Leather Tribe members are LGBTQ but this term is typically associated with the tribes in our community.

Lesbian – Although some Non-Binary individuals use this term to describe a non-man in a relationship with another non-man, the most common definition of lesbian is a woman who is sexually or romantically attracted to other women.

Lesbian Bed Death – A relationship that is all-in at the start but won't last forever.

Lesbian Labrys – A Labrys is a double-headed axe which was used as a weapon by the Amazons in mythology. Many years later, the Labrys started to be used as a symbol of empowerment for the lesbian community in the 1970's.

Lesbophobia – This term comprises various forms of negativity toward lesbians as individuals, as couples, or as a social group. Based on the categories of sex, gender, sexual orientation, lesbian identity, and gender expression; this negativity encompasses prejudice, discrimination, and abuse, in addition to attitudes and feelings ranging from disdain to hostility. As such, lesbophobia is sexism against women that intersects with homophobia.

LGBTQ – This is the short version of the full community's acronym, LGBTQQIP2SAA. Most times, you will find our community members use LGBTQ or LGBT to summarize the overall community in their speeches or everyday life. The overall acronym stands for:

L	Lesbian
G	Gay
B	Bisexual
T	Transgender
Q	Queer
Q	Questioning
I	Intersex
P	Pansexual
2S	Two-Spirit
A	Asexual
A	Aromantic

Librafluid – A person who is mostly Agender but also has a connection to masculinity and femininity that fluctuates between them.

Lifestyle Choice – An offensive term used to describe LGBTQ people's sexual orientation, gender expression and gender identity as a "choice."

Lipstick Lesbian – Usually refers to a lesbian with a feminine gender expression. Can be used in a positive or a derogatory way, depending on who is using it. It is sometimes also used to refer to a lesbian who is seen as automatically passing for heterosexual.

Lithosexual – This is a sexual orientation where the person feels sexual attraction to others but does not want a sexual relationship with them.

Lithromantic – This is a romantic orientation where the person feels romantic attraction to others but does not want a romantic relationship with them.

M

M-Spec – This term describes people who are sexually or romantically attracted to more than one gender. This could be Bisexual, Trisexual, Pansexual, etc. but it means a person is attracted to two or more gender identities.

MAAB / FAAB – These acronyms stand for "Male Assigned at Birth" and "Female Assigned At Birth" respectively. These terms are preferable to some more commonly used ones like "born male" or "born female." which are both derogatory ways to describe someone's gender assigned at birth.

Makkunrai – A gender identity in the Bugis society for women or feminine aligned gender identities.

Manflux – Someone whose gender identity is male or masculine aligned but whose gender fluctuates in intensity over any length of time.

Mascromantic – A person who is romantically attracted to males or masculine aligned gender identities.

Mascsexual – A person who is sexually attracted to males or masculine aligned gender identities.

Master-Slave – The relationship between two consenting adults who choose to take on dominant and submissive roles in either their sexual activity or in everyday life.

Maverique – A Non-Binary gender identity where the person feels a gender is present but that gender is not male, female, neutral, nor anything that comes close to those genders.

Microlabel – This term refers to a hyper specific subgroup in a larger community. For example, in the gay community we have Bears, Otters, Twinks, etc. These are ultra-specific labels that people in the LGBTQ can give themselves rather than being classified in the broader lesbian, gay, transgender, bisexual, or queer communities.

Military Tribe – A person who is part of a country's military and the LGBTQ. For example, someone could be attracted to others who wear military uniforms and are members of the armed forces.

Minority Stress – This describes the well documented and chronically high levels of stress faced by members of stigmatized minority groups. It may be caused by a number of factors, including poor social support and low socioeconomic status. Well understood causes of minority stress are interpersonal prejudice and discrimination.

Minus18 – While some people might read this term and automatically jump to the wrong conclusion, Minus18 is an LGBTQ charity in Australia working to improve the lives of LGBTQ youth. Our community in the LGBTQ have nothing to do with Minor Attracted Individuals and do NOT support them in any way.

Misgender – To refer to someone using a word (especially a pronoun or form of address) that does not correctly reflect the gender with which they identify.

Misogynoir – An unwarranted and hyper-specific hatred and distrust towards women of color. The term is nicknamed 'where racism and sexism meet'.

Mispronoun – The act of knowingly or unknowingly using the wrong pronouns to address someone. Usually this is done to undermine the validity of their gender and to bully transgender individuals.

Mixed Pronouns – This term describes when someone chooses pronouns they would like to be addressed by that do not commonly go together. For example: He/They or She/Him. It is a way of saying they use both sets of pronouns. In our examples, a person using He/They is a shorthand way of telling you they use both He/Him and They/Their pronoun combinations.

MLM / MSM – These categories are acronyms standing for Males who Love Males and Males who have sexual intercourse with Males respectively. These acronyms are often used in research and public health settings to collectively describe those who engage in same-sex sexual behavior, regardless of their sexual orientation.

Modifier – A word that changes the information about another word in the phrase. For example, someone who is transgender could tell you they are a trans-man. The "trans-" section of that phrase would be considered a modifier to the other information given. In our community, we use these terms so we can love and accept each other better. However, in the transphobic world, transphobic people use modifiers as an insult to transgender individuals. While having a conversation about your friend, they might say your friend is a trans-man. To the LGBTQ, we love and accept that fully but to a transphobic person, they are implying your friend is not a 'real' man since they are transgender. So, whether these are used as an affirmative word or meant in disrespect depends on the context and the person saying it.

MOGA – An acronym that stands for Marginalized Orientations and Gender Alignments which is used to describe the overall LGBTQ community.

MOGAI - An acronym that stands for Marginalized Orientations, Gender Alignments, and Intersex which is used to describe the overall LGBTQ community.

Mono-Lesbian – While Lesbian means a person of female or feminine aligned gender identity being attracted to other females or feminine aligned genders, Mono-Lesbian means a person of female or feminine aligned gender identity being attracted to only one gender identity, usually their own gender.

Monogamous – Two people who are sexually active with each other and do not have any outside sexual partners. For example, not an open or polyamorous relationship.

Monolith – The false belief that everyone in a community is the same and should be treated the same. For example, some people outside the LGBTQ community believe that all Lesbian, Gay, and Bisexual people are also Transgender. We in the community know this to be false but under the Monolith belief, all of our community members have the same sexual orientation, gender identity, and should be treated the same.

Monoromantive – The romantic attraction to only one gender but no more than one.

Monosexism – Usually aimed against bisexuals, this is the false belief that a person can only be physically attracted to one gender at a time and cannot be attracted to two or more genders simultaneously.

Monosexual – The sexual attraction to only one gender but no more than one.

MTF / M2F – These acronyms stand for Male to Female and describe a transgender person whose gender identity is female but they were assigned male at birth. Usually, it is the transgender person who will describe themselves using these acronyms.

MTX / M2X – These acronyms stand for Male to gender-expansive. They describe a genderqueer or gender-expansive person assigned male at birth.

Multigender – This term describes individuals who have more than one gender identity either at the same time or over any length of time.

Multisexual – A person who has more than one sexual orientation either at the same time or over any length of time.

NB – An abbreviated way to say Non-Binary.

NBi - Another abbreviated way to say Non-Binary.

Neopronoun – A set of pronouns commonly used by Non-Binary individuals that better and more accurately describe gender identities outside of the binary. For example: he, she, they, one, and it.

Neptunic – This term describes the sexual attraction from a Non-Binary individual to a female or person with a feminine aligned gender identity.

Neurogender – A term used to describe when a person's gender identity is directly linked to their neurodivergence.

Neutrois – Sometimes used interchangeably with Agender, Neutrois typically refers to a Non-Binary gender identity where there is a lack of gender felt by an individual.

Nibling – A gender-neutral term for niece/nephew.

Non-Binary – A person who identifies as Non-Binary feels their gender identity cannot be defined using the gender binary of male or female. Their gender is somewhere else on the gender spectrum but not Agender.

Non-Binary Bisexual – A person whose gender identity is outside of the gender binary and somewhere else on the gender spectrum and who is also sexually attracted to two genders, one of which could be their own gender.

Nonamorous – This term describes a type of relationship that does not include any long-term or intimate partnerships. People who are Nonamorous only have short-term relationships.

Norm – Short for "Normal", this is the expectation that everyone must be straight, cisgender, and not ever question their sexual orientation or gender identity as to not break the "norm" or the normal mold of what society thinks everyone should be.

Normative – Similar to *Norm*, this term describes the actions of society where sometimes people think everyone should be straight and cisgender. Normative describes the actions some people take in order to ensure everyone fits into the Norm instead of questioning their gender identity or sexual orientation.

Noun-pronouns – A word used to describe someone or something without using common pronouns. For example: rather than saying "My teacher took attendance. Then she had us open our books." Using Noun-pronouns, you would instead say "My teacher took attendance. The teacher then had us open our books." Typically, you can simply use the same words again or use the person's name in replace of specific pronouns like he, she, or they. This is a great way to address someone if you don't know what pronouns they prefer to be addressed by.

Omni – An abbreviated way to say "All".

Omni-Lesbian – A person who is both *Omnisexual* and *Lesbian.*

Omniromantic – A person who is romantically attracted to all genders at the same time.

Omnisexual – A person who is sexually attracted to all genders at the same time.

Opposite Sex – A term mostly used by transphobic individuals who have the false belief that there are only two genders. Rather than saying they are attracted to a person of another gender identity than their own (heterosexual), they will say they are attracted to the opposite sex. They do this to equate the terms gender and sex even though they are scientifically not the same at all and one does not describe the other. And they do this because saying the word "opposite" implies that there are only two options to choose from…but obviously we know there are millions of genders to choose from when sexually or romantically being attracted to other people.

Oraone – A gender identity in the Bugis society for males or masculine aligned gender identities.

Orbisian – This term is a Non-Binary sexual orientation referring to the attraction to women or people of feminine aligned gender identities.

Orientation – In simple terms, Orientation describes who you are attracted to. There are seven spectrums of Orientation including Physical, Sexual, Mental, Sensual, Aesthetical, Romantic, and Emotional. Each of these seven define how we are attracted to others including romantic partners, sexual partners, friends, and even family.

Otter – A person in the LGBTQ community who has a lot of body hair; however, unlike a *Bear*, Otters have a smaller body frame and weight.

Otter Tribe – This term is used to describe the overall community of people who are *Otters*.

Out – A term used to describe someone who is out of the closet and open about their sexual orientation or gender identity.

Outing – The deliberate or accidental sharing of another person's sexual orientation or gender identity without their explicit consent. Outing is disrespectful and presents a danger for many LGBTQ individuals which is why outing someone else should never be done. It is that person's information to share, whether or not you think that person is Out and open to everyone or not.

Ownership – A sub-group in the LGBTQ community where one individual in a relationship (generally a long-term relationship) is owned by their partner. For two consenting adults, this could be as simple as a *Master-Slave* relationship in sexual actions; but for more complex relationships, this could be the ownership of their partner full-time. For example, rather than promising someone you will be in a *monogamous* relationship with them and will never cheat on them, you could have an agreement between you both that says you own their body and they own yours.

Pan-Lesbian – A female or person whose gender identity is feminine aligned who is sexually attracted to others regardless of gender but has a heavy preference for other females or those whose gender identity is feminine aligned.

Pangender – A person who feels they cannot label their gender as male or female.

Panromantic – A person who is romantically attracted to others regardless of their gender.

Pansexual – A person who is sexually attracted to others regardless of gender. A great way to think about this term is to imagine a dating app on your phone. While gay males would look at a dating profile and make sure the person they are interested in is another male, lesbians would look to make sure the person is a female, and bisexuals would look to make sure the person is one of the genders they are attracted to; Pansexual people on the other hand won't care or bother to look at this section. No matter the gender identity in this box on a dating profile, they could still be interested in a relationship with that person.

Pansexual Demiromantic – A person who is sexually attracted to others regardless of gender; however, they are only romantically attracted to another person once an emotional bond is formed.

Partner – This is a gender-neutral term for a significant other and used often in the LGBTQ community rather than saying boyfriend or girlfriend. For example, if you were to ask a person if they have a boyfriend, you would be assuming they are gay or straight but if you asked them if they have a partner, you are not assuming their sexual orientation or their partner's gender identity and thus, respecting their relationship.

Passing – The act of presenting as cisgender or gender-typical, which is generally accomplished through conforming to gender roles. People may try to pass in anti-LGBTQ+ environments to ensure their safety. People who pass as straight or cis have the choice to either talk about their LGBTQ+ experience or to "fit in" to a cis- and hetero-normative world. Passing is not required for LGBTQ+ people to deserve respect and love.

PGPs – This acronym stands for someone's preferred gender pronouns. It is a term that simply describes the pronoun or set of pronouns that an individual would like others to use when talking to or about that individual.

Pillow Princess – A person who receives a lot more than gives in a sexual relationship.

Pink Triangle – First used as a symbol of hatred and discrimination towards LGBTQ people in Nazi Germany during World War II, the Pink Triangle is usually seen in an upside-down fashion with one point on the equilateral triangle facing down and two points on the top (like an arrow pointing down). The symbol has since been reclaimed by the LGBTQ community as a symbol of pride and you can now find the symbol on many Pride flags worldwide.

Polyamory – This term describes a person who has multiple romantic relationships simultaneously.

Polygender – Another term for Multigender, this term describes someone who has multiple genders at the same time or over any length of time.

Polysexual – A person who is attracted to many gender identities at the same time. This is not the same as Bisexual (since that definition is restricted to being attracted to two genders) or Trisexual (since that is restricted to three genders).

Pomoromantic – A person who does not fit into any particular label or kind of romantic attraction or someone who denies having romantic attraction.

Positive – This is a shortened version of saying someone is Positive for HIV / AIDS. People who identify as Positive are often very proud and even have their own Pride flag for showing their pride in being positive. While there is no cure yet for HIV (as of this writing in 2023), you can control it with treatment and you cannot catch HIV or AIDS by simply talking to someone so if you see their Pride flag or hear someone talking about being positive, please don't run away.

Post-Exposure Prophylaxis – Generally abbreviated as PEP, this refers to the process by which a person takes anti-HIV medications to prevent the chance of becoming HIV positive. This process is started as soon as possible after a person has possibly been exposed to HIV which is why it is so important for someone who is sexually active to go for regular STI testing.

Post-Op – A trans-identified person who has received Gender Affirming Surgery or Sexual Reassignment Surgery.

Pre-Op – A trans-identified person who has not received Gender Affirming / Sexual Reassignment Surgery and a term that implies that the person does intend to receive such surgical procedures. However, being pre-op does not diminish the validity of their gender in any way.

Preference – This term is often used by homophobic individuals trying to undermine and discriminate against homosexual, bisexual, and other sexualities beyond heterosexual (straight). Calling a type of attraction, a 'preference' implies it is a choice we are making to be attracted to the person we are with or want to be with. The new and much more inclusive term is *Orientation*.

Pronouns – Words used to describe something or someone that is being talked about (He, She, They, It, This, and That).

PTP – This acronym stands for a Person with a Transgender Parent, also sometimes called *Transpawn*.

Pup Tribe – Sometimes referred to as Puppies or Pup Play, the Pup Tribe are members of the LGBTQ community that love playing cute, cuddling, kissing (especially with tongue), and most times like being submissive in their sexual actions or in everyday life. Sometimes their partners are referred to as 'Owners' or 'Handlers'. Unlike Bears or Otters, Pups are not defined by their outward appearance like hair or body type. Members of this tribe almost always self-identify as being members of the tribe.

QPOC – An acronym that stands for Queer Person of Color or Queer People of Color.

QTPOC – An acronym that stands for Queer and Transgender People of Color.

Queer – Most times referred to as an all-inclusive term, Queer describes any sexual orientation or gender identity other than heterosexual (straight) and cisgender.

Queerbaiting – A marketing technique in which media creators or executives allude to the presence of LGBTQ+ characters or relationships within their content, but fail to include actual representation so as not to lose non-LGBTQ+ viewers.

Queerplatonic – Sometimes abbreviated as QPR, a Queerplatonic Relationship is one which goes beyond the normal confines of a platonic relationship (for example: two friends having sexual intercourse) but would not be described as a romantic relationship.

Queerspawn – A person with one or more LGBTQ+ parent or caregiver. Typically, this is a term used for self-identification.

Questioning – The process of exploring and figuring out your gender identity or sexual orientation before coming out to yourself or others.

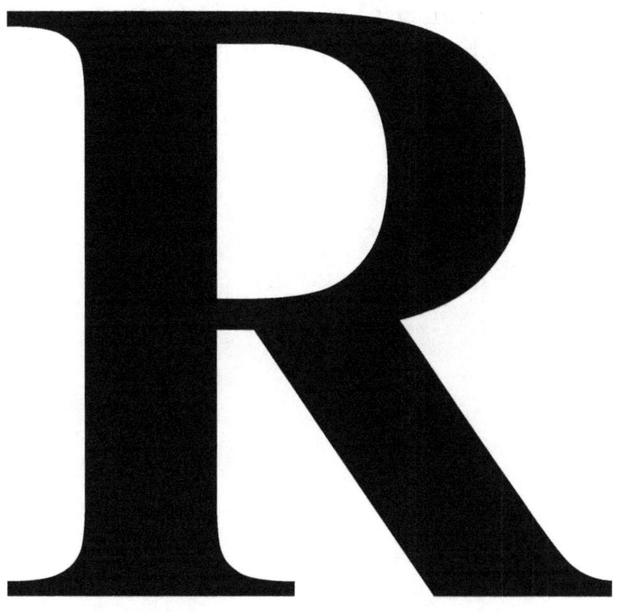

Rubber – Usually referred to as the Rubber Tribe or Rubber Pride, this community enjoys wearing or enjoys being with those who wear rubber clothing including shirts, pants, harnesses, or full-body suits during sexual endeavors. Not everyone that is a member of this community is also a member of the LGBTQ community but it is a term sometimes heard in the adult LGBTQ world.

Safe Space – This term is used to describe a place people can be comfortable expressing themselves without fear as it relates to their sexual orientation or gender identity.

Same-Gender Loving – This is another term to describe homosexuality of someone being sexually or romantically attracted to others of the same gender. Usually the term Same-Gender Loving is used in the African-American community.

Sapphic – Drawn from the Greek lesbian poet Sappho's name, this is a term used to refer to lesbian, bisexual, pansexual, or otherwise same-gender loving women.

Sex – Activity between two or more consenting individuals as the culmination of sexual attraction.

Sex Assigned at Birth – The two main categories given to humans at the time of their birth by doctors usually determined by a person's genitalia. These two categories are male and female; however, they have absolutely no association with what gender the person is.

Sex Change – This term is the extremely old and derogatory way of referring to Gender Reassignment Surgery. Also known as GRS, the term Gender Reassignment Surgery is used by some medical professionals to refer to a group of surgical options that alter a person's biological sex. "Gender confirmation surgery" is considered by many to be a more affirming term. In most cases, one or multiple surgeries are required to achieve legal recognition of gender variance. Some refer to different surgical procedures as "top" surgery and "bottom" surgery to discuss what type of surgery they are having without having to be more explicit.

Sexual Orientation – The emotional, romantic, or sexual feelings toward other people or no people on the 7 spectrums of attraction. While sexual activity involves the choices one makes regarding behavior, one's sexual activity does not define one's sexual orientation.

Sexual Preference – A derogatory term used to describe someone's sexual orientation; however, the word preference implies that the person makes the conscious choice to be gay, bisexual, pansexual, and so on.

SGL – This term is used as an alternative to the terms gay and lesbian. SGL is an acronym which stands for same-gender loving and the term is more commonly but not exclusively used by members of the African American and Black community.

Skolioromantic – A person who is romantically attracted to people who are transgender or Non-Binary.

Skoliosexual – A person who is sexually attracted to people who are transgender or Non-Binary.

Sodomite – A derogatory term used by those who hate the LGBTQ community to describe homosexual acts while at the same time calling those actions sinful in the eyes of their religion. One thing we will note here is that homosexual acts are not a sin in any major religion of the world.

SOGI – This acronym stands for Sexual Orientation and Gender Identity. It is typically used as a shorthand in writing and is rarely pronounced out loud.

SSA – This is an acronym which means Same Sex Attraction. This term is used to describe the experience of a person who is emotionally and/or sexually attracted to people of the same gender. Individuals using this term may not feel comfortable using the language of sexual orientation (For example: gay, lesbian, and bisexual) for personal reasons. Use of this term is not indicative of a person's sexual behavior. It is used most commonly in religious communities.

Stereotype – An incorrect idea or belief society has for a group of people. When referring to the LGBTQ community, common stereotypes are that we all dress a certain way or that we have a gay voice which does not exist seeing that straight people have the same higher tones in their voices sometimes.

Stud – While in the rest of the world, the word stud refers to a masculine person looking gorgeous, in the LGBTQ community stud could also refer to a butch woman or Non-Binary person who is black or *Latinx*.

Switch – Sometimes referred to as "Vers" or Versatile, this term describes a person's desire and ability to either top or bottom during intercourse with their partner in a gay relationship.

T4T – This acronym stands for Transgender person looking for another Transgender person. Trans 4 Trans. You might see this acronym on a dating profile most often where a transgender person is seeking a relationship with another transgender individual.

TERF – This is another term to describe a transphobic person or someone that falsely believes that transgender people do not exist. A TERF believes (with no science or evidence to back their claims by the way) that transgender women do not have a legitimate gender identity and are extremely hostile and discriminatory towards transgender people for these beliefs.

TGNC – This acronym is used to describe the initialism for trans and gender nonconforming and is merely an abbreviation of Trans Gender and Non-Conforming. It is an umbrella term for people who are not cisgender. It is pronounced T-G-N-C, but is more commonly written than spoken.

Thirst Trap – Posting something sexy just to get someone to notice you. This term is often used to describe a profile picture on a dating or hookup app like Grindr or the far superior Howlr.

Throuple – A relationship between three individuals of any gender identity combination.

Top – This term describes a person's desire and ability to penetrate their partner during intercourse in a gay relationship.

Top Surgery – Surgery performed on an individual's chest and breasts area as a part of gender-affirming surgery. For Female Assigned at Birth people, this can be a chest reduction or a full removal. For Male Assigned at Birth people, this can be an increase in chest size using saline or silicone.

Tranny – A derogatory term usually used by a transphobic person who hates the transgender community and is used to describe a transgender person in a negative way.

Trans-antagonistic – Antagonistic means to provoke or seek out a fight with someone so Trans-angtagonistic means to seek out a fight and to provoke a fight with transgender people. Usually this is done by transphobic individuals who want to harm the transgender community in some way.

Transcestors – An informal term for trans elders, coming from a combination of the words "transgender" and "ancestors." The term highlights the fact that many trans people do not get to grow old. The term also celebrates inter-generational relationships. Trancestors can be well-known within the movement or personal to a community, filling a parent or grandparent-like role. Trancestors can also make an impact during and after their lives and prove that there is a long history of transgender people throughout the world.

Transgender – This is an umbrella term which describes individuals whose *gender identity* or *gender expression* does not match their *sex-assigned at birth*.

Transition – The process of changing a person's *gender expression* to match their *gender identity*.

Transitioning – This term describes the action of *Transition*. For example: a trans-man would cut their hair shorter and start wearing clothing more closely aligned with masculine clothing.

Transpawn – A person who has one or more transgender or Non-Binary parent.

Transphobia – The fear of, discrimination against, or hatred of transgender or gender non-conforming people or those who are perceived as such.

Transsexual – A very old and outdated term to describe transgender people who have undergone surgery or medical transition of some kind to match their gender expression with their gender identity. The term transsexual is no longer used in any facet of the LGBTQ community as it has now been replaced by the much more inclusive term, transgender.

Trigender – A person who has three gender identities either simultaneously or over any length of time.

Tucking – The process of hiding one's penis and testes with tape, tight shorts, or specially designed undergarments.

Twink Tribe – First originated from the popular bakery treat called Twinkies, the Twink Tribe is a sub-group of the gay and bisexual communities. Most of the time, other members of the community describe someone as a Twink and this title is not self-imposed. Twinks are described as younger and typically very skinny members of the gay and bisexual communities. Much like the bakery treat, Twinks are light and airy on the outside, meaning they are not very educated. Also like the bakery treat, Twinks have a creamy center which is typically the only thing Twinks are associated with for doing well…sexual intercourse and the creamy center is the end result of that. Some use the term as a derogatory one but most of the time, it is used in a positive and affirmative manner that many Twinks use proudly as a badge of honor.

Two-Spirit – A contemporary term that connects today's experiences of LGBT Native American and American Indian people with the traditions from their cultures.

U-Haul – A term used to describe someone who is investing too quickly into a relationship and ready to move in with their partner right away.

Unicorn (Couple) – When used in the setting of a straight couple, this term refers to a couple looking for a bisexual person to be their third partner in a threesome act of intercourse.

Unicorn (Gay) – When used in the setting of a gay man in a relationship with another gay man, this term is a code word to describe the one man's desire for sex in that moment. For example, if my husband and I were in the company of friends and I had the desire to leave the party to have special time with him, I might try to find a natual way in our conversation to say the code word "unicorn". This way my husband would know I was in the mood for intercourse without our friends knowing what's happening.

Urge to Merge – Often used by lesbians more often than gay men, this term describes a person who rushes to marriage in a relationship.

Vers / Versatile – Sometimes referred to as being a *Switch*, this term describes a person's desire and ability to either top or bottom during intercourse with their partner in a gay relationship.

Voguing – The act of using exaggerated hand gestures to tell a story in gender performances by a Drag Queen or King. These performances get their name from the popular fashion magazine, Vogue.

Vore – The rare sexual attraction or fetish of the idea of being swallowed or devoured by someone or something else.

WLW / WSW – These acronyms stand for Women Loving Women and Women who have Sex with other women respectively. These terms refer to lesbian, bisexual, pansexual, or otherwise same-gender loving women. They are often used in communities of color. As more understandings of sexuality have come to light, WLW has largely replaced lesbian as a unifying term to describe these women.

Zi / Hir – These are alternate pronouns that are gender neutral and preferred by some transgender people. They replace "he" and "she" and "his" and "hers" respectively.